True Winds Travel Poems

A Journey through Seven Continents

by Trudy Wendelin

First Edition 2025
Copyright © 2025 Trudy Wendelin
Written by Trudy Wendelin
Cover Art and Design by Nicole Monahan.
ISBN 979-8-218-65097-1

To the Traveler in All of Us…

"You cannot travel the path until you have become the path itself." -Buddha

Contents: Travel Poems from 7 Continents

North America 73

Asia

"It's better to travel well,
than to arrive." - Buddha

The Wisdom Path
Po Lin Monastery, Hong Kong

From nimbus blue
shrine, upon mountainside
a rock blooms into nirvana…
Buddha speaks
through rustling trees
and rosewood pillars with scriptures
on Heart Sutra's eightfold
path, interbeing
above a sparkling sea.

I walk the Path of Infinity,
as above, so below on 8
with empty mind
in bright transparency,
detached, as a wing's feather
feeling everything
arise from nothing…

I am a silent traveler
resonating to mystic hues
on this deep sojourn
in yin stillness, as light
moves my heart's blood.
All senses become one
insight, from which I perceive
spontaneously a spark to walk
in harmony with the fire.
Each step, attuned to a pulse
flows in pure freedom

with compassion,
feeling no desire for sun's
golden warmth or
moon's silver rays.

My essence in cadence
with the earth's middle way
walks peripatetic truth
from each step as a mantra
for *Samadhi to become the path itself…

*Samadhi – State of meditative consciousness in Buddhism

Taiwanese Tea Ceremony

A fragrant array
of dark green leaves,
fermented to elegance
in nuances on bamboo tray.
The poised teapot's
hot water extracts essence
in taste and light, filling
delicately, a cup. In humble
room at wood table,
I mindfully sip
in a sensual limbo, connecting
with subtle mouthfeel
and tongue swirling, feeling
the moment flow deep
into my root of being.
Waft of flowery scent
in hints of flavor
pure as a mountain
fills my hearth from
tea's healing vibrance.

Japanese Cherry Blossoms

Soft hues bloom in pink
clouds and fragrant breeze…
as the aesthetic healing. Mirage
harmonizes blood, white and rose
nuances of spring, among children
laughing in mint green leaves…
painting a pastel dream. Zen
sky whispers haikus upon
floral loft, vulnerable to
windy bough shade.

Petals fall like pink snow
awaiting sweet-red cherries.

Tao of Taiwan's Taroko Gorge

The *Tao is an artist
of ancient landscapes,
lush and majestic in splendor
as the sky is vast.

From deep bedrock
the limestone morphs into
white-silver and black marble mountains
as nature grandly rises...

Chimerical stones
and sun in wind's
fire swirling dawn
awaken from crevasse of light

a painting, framed
by haze of crimson clouds.
The turquoise river
erodes silhouettes to time

along the mosaic edge,
sculpting a magnum
opus as shamanic deities
dance the forces of Yin & Yang.

I etherize into *Wu Wei sky
among stone canyons, intuitively
soaring in Swallows Grotto
as fresh squall aloft.

On lonely mountainside,
Eternal Spring Shrine
immortalizes ancestors'
holy death by tears

from rock ridge stillness,
as thunderclap echoes
the monsoon falling
light of waterdrops, sparkling

qi vapors on earth.
Evergreen trees and seasons
balance the dragon pine
and red autumn leaves.

The Tao is an artist
in wind, water and time
as elements of nature's Muse
shapeshifting rocks and clouds into myth.

*Tao – Natural way of universe in East
Asian philosophy
*Wu Wei – Effortless action aligned
with the Tao

Walk in Nepal's Agricultural Nirvana
for Acupuncture Relief Project

Through bitter-yellow mustard fields
I wander the terraces…
along steep passages, narrow edges,
over makeshift stone bridges and irrigation
walls in lush, ephemeral harvest
of potatoes, cauliflower and wheat
from Himalayan dirt.

Gingerly, I balance my gait
on slender ledge, then hollow step
and cross over into a veranda
where visceral gold, green
and indigo penetrate my bones…

On the path's horizon, surprised,
I notice my favorite elderly patient
walking towards me. Her face lights up
with a heartfelt, raspy "NAMASTE!"
Ahh, the word of infinite worlds:
the divine and self is same in you and me.
In sky blue dress, wrinkled-tan skin
and wind-electric hair…she's wildly
organic, like an outgrowth of the land,
where pretention is extinct
and only sun, air and water matter.

She loudly talks fast Nepali.
I understand through the language barrier,
her sincere expression of light.
With a mischievous grin, she reaches
underneath a patuka, wrapped endlessly
around her petit waist,
inside a hidden pocket, handing me
pieces of crumbled, homemade bread.
I appreciate her blood and flour.

Graciously, she lifts her walking stick,
guiding her two gentle, grazing
water buffalos out of my path.
I wave good-bye, humbled
and greater than I was before.

Thailand's Wooden Sanctuary of Truth
"Truth is One; Paths are many." – Gandhi

On the horizon of mysterious cape
rises a wood mountain with spires
impaling the sun's heart,
as golden tones of wind mantras
glow upon clouds shapeshifting light.

Mirror in nirvana reflects the truth
of ethereal wood sculpting prayers
from braille symbols on Buddhist shrines
as a spiritual muse
for the breath of humanity.

This papyrus for Gods and Goddesses
inspires a mystic Renaissance
of sacred designs and crystalizes meditation:
the 4 noble truths manifest as
air, earth, fire and the sea…

into surreal mindscape, trusting
a deep path rising
amidst collage of gothic theism
as blood and sap flow
in leaves of Shiva's branches.

The Tao is abyss from which
everything blooms, as I am a
hologram of all life: My desires
are blossoms wilting into a
moonless night of translucent qi.

I vibrationally dissolve
OBSTACLES into sylvan void
near the bronzed Ganesh, like
a new spirit with no bones or flesh,
just a hollow wing on earth.

The Truth enlightens all paths
into heart of Kuan Yin
as a crystal fire
opens to omnipotence, so peace
ignites sparks into one flame.

Ha Long Bay "Bay of Descending Dragons"
Healing Remembrance of Vietnam War

From white clouds morph
descending blue dragons, alchemical
as the wind and sun, dropping
jade, like healing bombs.
Nightmare's glitter, incandescent in
a secret water grotto,
with agent orange as a dye
from nature's omnipotence.
Ancient rainforests cleanse
a decade's decadence
in sun's humid breeze
as tropical breath.
The limestone mountain's
rocky tide, like a heart
from metallic shrapnel,
bleeds the past, submerged
in green shadows.
Moonlit napalm fog
transforms a generation
of proxied memories
doused by cooling bay in jade islands…

Maldivian Diva

On Indian Ocean
a tropical nirvana engulfs
coral islands and atolls
into spiral archipelago. Teal
swells inundate submarine
sky of bubbles. Surreal safari
flows in stream to crystal reefs,
fragile as underwater glass.

I swim the tidal calm
diving into water silk abyss.
Among flying manta rays
and undulating eels, I glide
like a wave over kaleidoscope of
schools. A clear current
moves the angelfish, turtles and
quiet barracuda. At night
the bioluminescent plankton glows
a blue-green sea of stars.

Resurfacing…
I remember foam and moon's
warm coral bleaching
in sea horizon rising
over extinct volcanoes.

Nagasaki's Origami Clouds
Never Forget August 9, 1945

A harbinger for peace
whispers upon sparkling
harbor and green mountains in
origami rainbow clouds,
as my day to not forget

at Ground Zero
empowered by prayer,
I invoke Buddha and Shinto Gods'
forgiveness and infinity
for atomic, nightmare screams…

under ominous sky
encrypted from metallic sun
as satanical heat,
vaporizing children and soft
flowers into scorched riverbed.

Nuked flesh and skin
peeled off bones, with terror
combusting hearts from
helpless ashes to angels,
remembered by moon.

Armageddon blasts
of radioactive windstorms
murdered innocence and hope;
a soul loss, excavated
from nuclear wasteland.

Samurai sword eerily
smelted to smoke
upon dead moonscape,
with a black fetus
charred in blood shadows.

Today, mothers raise your children
with the cranes' wings,
where posterity flies freely
in paper blue sky
floating on origami clouds…

Catching the Bullet Train in Kyoto

White sci-fi locomotive
approaching, streamlined eloquence
precisely on time in Kyoto
aerodynamic movement, slick & efficient
no resistance, humming
streak of opaque windows...
jittery anticipation as
screeching scratches my bare skin,
feeling draft from white speed through bones
static hair, flying
electric blue stripe whizzing by
braking into a still life.
Japanese announcements, swiftly
ricochet in all directions
of terminal, whitewashed with no garbage,
starkly clean, I smell nothing.
Sliding doors dart open...
Quickly, I step inside sleek motion
as foreigner, travelling in stream-of-consciousness,
sitting and observing pink, blurry windows
cherry blossom epitaphs
behind, till I softly notice
a tidy family in reserved seats.
They sit in front of me. I can't not watch
a stern mother with long, shiny-black
hair & well-mannered children.
The little boy & girl silently nod at each other.
Simultaneously, all three remove lids
from neat bento boxes, gingerly
then lift the wasabi sushi
with red-tipped bamboo chopsticks
to their hungry lips.

Haiku Trilogy

A cherry blossom's
pink cloud lingers on green hill
awakened by gold.

Origami crane
on rainbow cloud under sun
floating peacefully.

Warm noodles fill heart
with a delicious feeling
to know spicy thought.

Oceania

"Traveler, there are no paths.
Paths are made by walking."
-Aboriginal Proverb

Uluru's Red *Dreamtime

There's an Aboriginal *songline, a sky
journey through the Pleiadian star stream
into a constellation of light, illuminating
footprints of ancestors across the land.
From ochre dawn to dusk at high noon
the heart centre is an infernal vortex
dreaming my walkabout...

Alone, in a sea of spinifex grass
and winds on secret bedrock,
I find the lonely inselberg endures
morphing shapes of time.
Sandstone, feldspar and quartz compose
*Anangu songs of minerals
carved by creative winds and water,
painted with the palette of iron
an epitaph for red stone,
embedded in lithospheres
with shadows of rust composition.

Ephemeral strata of time
root eternity into a moment
with ancient, infrared layers.
Sediments deposit periods
from millennia of rainfall in
alluvial fans and fluvial channels
to compose geology in Outback,
connecting sky and earth.

In dreamtime, I observe
landscapes of chimerical beings
shapeshift into sky…
with petrified waves of stillness
and creatures that die screaming
in eternal night, as fossils
sculpt ether spirits to stone.

Aboriginal ancestors sustain
desert fauna of red kangaroo
and reptilian cold blood,
below rainbow clouds of lavender,
honey grevillea and pink everlastings.
Mulga dreaming boomerang
flies on emu's wing, returning to
bloodwood shield
under desert oak shade,
as spinifex spreads across dry fields
my bush medicine and desert bloom.

*Dreamtime – Aborigines connected with
creation powers for divine intervention
*Songline – Dreamtime spirits' trails that
connect sacred sites
*Anangu – Native owners of Uluru

Stone of *Dreamtime
Ochre Pits, Australia

In raw, ochre realms
Aborigines paint the blood
of ancestors from deep palette's
minerals onto desert landscapes

as shadow of sienna
fades into glowing winds
through the ephemeral light
with singed whispers of fire,

mining emotions from eternity,
excavating years from eons
of ancient tears and flesh
into dense moment.

My heart resonates with
sanguine memories of death
and dry, earthen tones
upon pyre of mystic clay

in golden shards of day.
Dawn's horizon warms
the haze of russet hues,
tinged with iron rust

and rocks of spirit's viscera,
bloodletting dreaming tracks
with songs to sing into existence
my walkabout near a desert stream.

*Dreamtime - Aborigines
connected with creation powers for
divine intervention

Jenolan Caves, Australia
World's Oldest Cave System

Into catacomb of limestone
I find a cold chamber of shadows
and penetrate the deep mystery,
listening to an oracle of ancient
lithospheres, resounding their creation
stories, as petroglyphs to encrypt
secrets of dreamtime.

Stalactites drip minerals, downwards
stalagmites deposit, upwards
merging a grand column,
connecting body and spirit.

This is where I mine emotions
and communicate with aboriginal ancestors…

Dreamtime at Blue Lake, Australia

I intuitively listen to winds
and feel the aboriginal hues
along songlines, where the ethereal map
paints light green lands. Sage of beauty
haunts in eucalyptus trees' blue haze
as silver-white bark sheds
minty-sweet aromas
that refresh and clear the mind...
Mirror of water sky clouds
shatters thoughts like a kaleidoscope
in aquamarine mirage.

My walkabout of wisdom
deepens a cerulean melancholy
and cool shadows, lingering
where Rainbow Serpent veneer
soars toward amber sun...
as interlude for lonely spirits, aloft
with effervescent flesh.
The sylvan, tranquil lake
shimmers truth of limestone earth
with animism of rocks, trees and stars
through numinous mists,
as a strange, indigo dream
immersed in past, present and future
when the living and dead cocreate, eternally...

Crossing Tasman Sea

The teal horizon
opens a portal into a
twilit sky of orange-pink
shrouds, as maritime dreams
absorb essence of eucalyptus green
earth for omnipotence,
navigating the hues with
a sextant, imperiled,
by latitudes of roaring forties
among ultramarine seascapes.

Crescent moon rises
in dusky atmosphere revealing
Southern Cross.

New Zealand's Fiordland Trilogy

I. Milford Fiord

Long, long ago in the dawn of time
a crescendo of glacial lands
carved fiords, valleys and mountains
drifting on oceans as *Gondwana…
weathering cataclysmic myths
from the Milky Way's seasons, spiralling
a dreamscape into lost eternity.

Now, a majestic force of nature flows
in water labyrinth through
the humbling, steep canyon walls,
embedded with greenstone, garnet
and magnetic quartz of light
opening alpine meadows into clouds.
Infinite wilderness surrounds
as silver and red beech forests,
tree ferns, mossy granite
and snow-capped mountains
with aquamarine cataracts, falling
on shadows of time,
inspired by wafts of sea brine
and grounded into deep, watery past.

*Gondwana – Supercontinent comprised of
South America, Antarctica, Africa, Australia,
Zealandia and Indian subcontinent before
Continental Drift

II. Dusky Fiord

An interlude of damask
mists in dusky fiords
unveils coral pink apparitions
to paint the sunset.

A time portal suspends
with purpureal haze
softly over sunken day
in muse of a waking dream, till
horizon swallows the sun
as moon rises, esoterically,
into twilight sky.

III. Doubtful Fiord

Through remote water passages
an ancient oracle eerily flows
in currents of foggy winds,
lingering over lonely valley,
demystified by giant stone walls.

Aotearoa, the *Maori name for
"Land of the Long White Cloud"
reflects the surreal cloudscapes
on glassy waters in secret coves,
where the spindrift conceals
endangered black coral on seabed,
encrypted with cache mirrors.
Occult wisdom empowers
the sacred path into arcana
as the nomadic mystery maze...

At moon's low tide, overcast
by grey and silver clouds,
monoliths sink in deep chasms of doubt
with tears cascading, vulnerably
on wake of shadows and light,
Gothic as an ancient fiord.

*Maori - Indigenous Polynesian people of
New Zealand

Papua New Guinea Escape

In exotic sanctuary, enshrined
by volcanic rock and coral reefs,
I walk on tropical island
awestruck with Jurassic instincts.
Green tsunami spreads…
tectonic jungle under eruption
of blue lava and ashen clouds.

The whispering tree ferns
stand near equator as tinder
for Pacific Ring of Fire.
Pyroclastic shield volcano sleeps
and awakens in cycles
of magma rising.

A caldera and harbor
steam the mineral, healing baths
with eucalyptus winds and
red ginger. I experience
nature on brink of earthquake,
imminent like a storm, from
Mount Tavurvur and Vulcan.

Childlike, I smell frangipani
in otherworldly landscapes and lush
foliage with hibiscus eyes
for renewal of senses.
White-silver hair of *Tolai people
glistens in sun the robust health,
absorbing minerals and talismans
from fecund earth. I savor
their sweet coconut milk
for longevity.

On rim, overlooking cove…
the volcano hotspot enlightens
my surreal journey. Intense
flora and fauna root me
in raw, supernatural moment.

*Tolai – Native people of Papua New
Guinea

Antarctica

"I am hopeful that Antarctica in its symbolic robe of white will shine forth as a continent of peace as nations working together there in the cause of science set an example of international cooperation."   - Richard E. Byrd

Antarctica's "Lady in White"

There's a lonely countenance to the "Lady in White." Her pristine and infinite silence seduces all trespassers into a white vision of divinity. Frost bites from her icy stare, aloof and at home in extremities of noon darkness and midnight sun. Eerie quietude suspends as a twilit dream, lingering over a frozen desert, with snow as ancient as the earth. Thoughts freeze into oneness from the cold scream of silence, enveloping the mind into a deep trance of tranquility. Frigid air chills through vacant winds in time, luring all senses into a strange wasteland of beauty.

Her glassy waters reflect the tundra as a dreamscape to surreal lands, with glacial-blue icebergs drifting in solitude. The sun's obscure rays softly glow, as mountains submerge the sky into ghostly snow. The frostbitten muse of the "Lady in White" dances into a crystal horizon with no footprints. Her wan shadows haunt the clouds with wings of a soft mirage...

Elegant diamond moon
of white illusions finds
solitude in indigo winds
and snowy twilight,

Glittering in infinity,
transparent as air
reflecting glaciers
onto water mirrors.

A heart-numbing chill
freezes her lunar tide
into stillness, frostbitten
by love's pain.

A crevasse of visions
fills eons in a moment,
with the frozen star
over a lonely mountain.

Deep blue iceberg
cuts aloofly, her floating dream
with the ethereal truth
of death's edge.

At winter solstice, aurora
australis transmutes her
monotone into electric bloom
and dancing sky psychedelia.

Europe

"I met a lot of people in Europe.
I even encountered myself."
- James Baldwin

**Kos, Greece: Birthplace
of Hippocrates "Father of Medicine"**

From the mythic archipelago
Greek blue inspired miracles
in Aegean Sea, where
Cypress Groves and cicadas
sang the Hippocratic Oath.
I feel enamored
to be in the heart of history.
Epic Trojan War stories
at first hospital, a healing temple
invented our Father of Medicine.
The hot springs and mountains
dreamed a deep health rising
like Mediterranean democracy.

God of the Sun, Apollo
turned his son into
minerals, plants, amulets and spells
for Materia Medica. Holistic
ethics and moral compass
empowered high beliefs
in the Hippocratic Corpus,
to first do no harm
at the *Asclepieon sanctuary.

Three terraces rose to
Ionic and Doric Temples above
fuchsia bougainvillea & bubbling aqueducts.
This ancient vista crowned a beacon
for healing pilgrimages. In Kos town,
the peripatetic Hippocrates
taught under the Plane Tree
in cooling shade and
premeditated the physician template
for the Occidental world,
esteemed for millennia.
I leave the island, humbled
and deeper on my healing path.

*Asclepieon – Healing temple in ancient
Greece, dedicated to Asclepius

Gullfoss "Golden Falls"
To Sigridur Tomasdottir,
Iceland's OG Environmentalist

Deep in a canyon
flows the cold cascade
of water's bloom from
blue glacier melt, falling
into Icelandic riverbed.

Nature awakens the sky
whispering clouds
from a golden void,
glowing underground,
beneath the humbled stone.

Water prisms refract
a transparent arc
in spindrift light, deluged
by rainbow beams
and green shadows

in ionic motion
brightened by winds
from erosion of streams
and glittery showers,
vanishing into Earth.

The past and future
merge in glass cataracts
swirling mists
as sea crevasse
of a mossy, rock suture.

Now, is a feeling
of truth when effervescent
waters purify emotions
to let go and breathe
the clean essence.

Scotland's Isle of Skye

Alone in opalescent fog…
the sparkling colors
reverberate through my bones, healing
a path with no desires. I wander
authentically, allowing my magnetic senses
to find a current's flow, feeling
a full spectrum of being.
From white sky, I follow
the sun's golden mean into
glory, as it refracts me into the ether
aglow like a glass
ingenue, finding infinity…

Then, I feel my earth's green ground
in a soft limbo of being,
from which I hear the heath
manifesting my heart's song
upon grassy moorland sojourn.
Hues are a palette of the unknown, aligned
with mystic detours. I intuit
realms, with sun glinting through
my foggy past into bright moments.

Shetland Islands' Folklore

Through green mists, rocky shores emerge
from halo of mysterious lands…
emboldened by a glimpse of sun, the vast
seascape awakens all that listen to its waves
in the gothic winds, flying
over the earth's glowing haze, where I find
a veil of light, alone, on the edge of a cloud,
waning for the moon's subtle glare
when I sing to the mischievous sea *trow and dance
upon the shifting sands of life and death.

*trow- A mischievous folkloric fairy in Shetland and
Orkney Islands

Lanzarote -
Canary Island of 1,000 Volcanoes

I follow siroccos
to a volcanic moonscape.
Lichen-colored cones, calderas and
fissured basalt emerge from the
vast lava fields.

Minerals blend earthen
pigments of red, brown,
black, beige and rust. Innately, I
feel rugged sensations of a
landscape with cataclysmic stories.

The terrain is Gothic art, created
by nature from apocalyptic eruptions
molten for 6 years as the
infernal lava flow of
intense majesty.

Fire Mountain is a castle
with devil and pitchfork as king
of wasteland, abundant
with volcanic bombs, cooling
into sea of lacquered, lava waves.

Sculptures by Cesar Manrique
organically grow from land
in suspension of being, still
for manmade architecture to
express language of geology.

Perched on Mirador del Rio,
an epic escarpment of indigo
summit at basalt terrace, I overlook
the collage of sky and sea
emboldened by bright abyss.

Africa

"I never knew of a morning in Africa
when I woke up that I was not happy."
- Ernest Hemingway

Medina of Tunis

I walk through Bab al-Bhar Gate
bewildered by time-travel
into a fountain of Mediterranean, African
and Middle Eastern centuries.
My impulse is to get lost
amidst the waft of senses…
In a flash, I imagine saffron nuances
on my cinnamon tongue, swirling
a hookah pipe with wild thyme.
Medicinal herbs are wise
smudging sage incense,
as glass bottles of perfume
invoke a jasmine desire.
Curiously, I open Arabic blue door
into the goldsmith's mine,
embezzling gems from clouds,
realizing a souk is an escape
into cultural wilderness.
The artisan feels colors
painting a story on ceramic tiles
with silk interlude. I drink mint
tea for connection. The ritual
stimulates my third eye…
wandering the labyrinth of alleyways
while mused in de ja vu,
I laugh and find love
as ecstasy inside my heart!

Aloe Vera

Deep in the green
roots of life, I feel
cool inspirations soothe
my skin with serenity,
absorbing moisture
like an emerald cloud
glistening dewy gel
for health essence.

The plant of immortality
at Egyptian temples
found golden mean, with leaves
sprouting like the sun's rays.
From oasis sands
the desert sky blooms
below, a limelight mirage
gilded in new dawn.

ZANZIBAR

A wooden dhow sailboat, breezily
takes me through turquoise
archipelago, retracing intense history:
I open exotic Zanzibari door into
revolution of Swahili and Arabic spectacles
among cinnamon sun and nutmeg dirt
in Stone Town labyrinth...

Naively, I stroll among
cultural potpourri with the
zeitgeist of African spice trade.
Sweet vanilla incense wafts in humid
heat under black pepper clouds.
My tourist ego shops at Darajani Bazaar
for flowers, tanzanite and street food.
But, the rancid stench of fish,
squid and sharks catapult me
into Jaws Corner. Here, I laugh
among deep community under a tree
drinking Arab coffee, playing dominos
and speaking a foreign tongue.

Wandering alleyways, I sadly learn...
Arabic wooden doors, ostensibly
marked status for slaveowners
with carved chains, framing
doorway. Omani motifs
sculpted wood with frankincense trees,
lotus flowers, rosettes and date palms.
Tropical patterns engrave a baroque
passage with vines on lintel.

At Old Slave Market,
I hear tortured moans of ghosts,
crammed in dank-stone cell. I experience
stories of human carcasses. I feel
emancipation of African slave trade.
I offer silent prayer at memorial
for humanity in chains.

Off the beaten path…
a cacophony of fans swarm
birthplace of Freddie Mercury,
the British Queen of a rock band,
exiled by revolution. He will rock
you into Bohemian rhapsody for
a musical journey.

Finally, I shapeshift in raw nature
at Jozani Forest, exploring mahoganies,
baobab trees, mangroves and salt marshes.
Flora and fauna populate the bush
with neon centipedes and red colobus
monkeys, devouring bright berries.
Driving back to Stone Town, we sing
HAKUNA MATATA!

Namibia's Coastal Desert

Sand meets the sea
on high dunes with golden
waves of quartz. Stark
atmosphere bewilders at nomadic
crossing. I follow ridgeline stretching
eons from erosion and stones,
with sharp grains blowing, unabashedly
into my bloodshot sclera.

The skeleton coast is
a murky grave of crashing waves,
littered with shipwrecks and rocks.
Coral bones and dead flotsam
scatter on cold Atlantic seabed,
colliding with warm currents
into ghosts of maritime fog.
Mesmerized, I see a tsunami
of brown fur seals engulf the
cape in tide and moon.

Inland, a pink lake is
the mineral kaleidoscope of
salt and water. Flamingos
are a flamboyance, demure,
as the feathered shadow of a rose.

I discover deep folly
is science of evolutionary
moon, as vast escarpment
envelops rainclouds. Namib
coastal desert is a dense pattern
of geology in hot matrix.

African minerals embed
exotic tinctures for diamond
excavations. Deadpan maneuvers
like Apartheid are naturally extinct
to me and my friends.

South Africa's Cape of Good Hope

On a precipice, I recite the epic poem
Os Lusíadas with hope
from lighthouse on headland, feeling
winds in aquamarine maelstrom
of Antarctic and Mozambique currents.

I imagine sandstone promontory, jutting
into the seascape like a dragon
swirling mythical vortexes
for 1,000 shipwrecks among
great white sharks, whales and seals.
Legend relives the sailor's curse
for eternity on Flying Dutchman
facing ferocious Cape of Storms.
The heroic odyssey circumnavigates
fog with compass to India,
where marine menagerie swims
in constellations of tide and moon.

Alongside, sea of grass undulates
waves on green lands, glistened
with gold King Protea flowers.
The oystercatcher and sunbird fly over
cape like light spraying from sun. Elands,
zebras and red hartebeest calmly graze
while the baboon crosses highway,
glaring into my camera lens.

Revelation of night's hope
is the Southern Cross, guiding
celestial whims as possibilities for deep
adventure into the mystical void
of my intense, nautical wanderlust.

Os Lusíadas – Epic Portuguese poem
published in 1572 about discovery of route
from Portugal, circumnavigating South
Africa to India

The Lemur

At dawn, a conspiracy
rises into
rainforest clouds.
Large terracotta eyes
embolden the sun.
Tree hollow is a lullaby.
The stealth is high
as afternoon falls
into green horizon.
Nocturnal species
delves the darkness
with tooth combs. This
Madagascar icon is a
hairy pollinator, making
everything regurgitate. The
matriarchal adaptation
smells an island, endemic
for unique patterns. Ring-
tailed primates, wet-nose
congeals fragrance
into time-lapse. This creature
sings a cappella, performing
stink fights from
wrist glands. Interacting
with a troop, seed
dispersers and vertical jumping
to soaring treetops.
Perpetual motion scurries
innocence, with pup
on back. Wild ear tufts
listen in bewilderment.
The cuteness is palpable.

However, their forest habitat
is a decibel. Floundering on
extinction amidst the hot
wasteland and machetes?
Without lemurs,
is this world worth livin' in?

South America

The Heights of Machu Picchu – Pablo Neruda

"Look at me from the depth of the earth,
laborer, weaver, silent shepherd:
tamer of wild llamas like spirit images:
construction worker on a daring scaffold:
waterer of the tears of the Andes:
jeweler with broken fingers:
farmer trembling as you sow:
potter, poured out into your clay:
bring to the cup of this new life
your old buried sorrows."

Galapagos Islands Journey

Amidst a majestic cataclysm
of ocean currents and volcanic eruptions
an archipelago emerged from the sea…
The supernatural diversity
is a menagerie of evolution.
There is no predatorial malice or fear.
Innocent castaways adapt to
organic elements of cacti, coral reefs and lava
rocks on cobalt blue ocean.

The Galapagos tortoise is
my power animal, retelling
me to slow down and be
AWAKE in the dream.
The mantra is longevity and
sacred, green earth.
I have arrived as a guest
to the true Animal Kingdom
among a kaleidoscope of survival,
in harmony where
species instinctively coexist,
outside human nature's fence.

Where else can I intuitively swim
with sea lions, sea turtles and sharks
among fish constellations?
Where else can I sit alongside a blue-footed booby
vulnerable with her nest and eggs?
Where else can I search the longing, sad
eyes of a sea lion pup?
Where else can I climb up to earth's

largest caldera and scry
our planets secret magma?
Where else at the equator can anyone
say hello to a playful penguin?

Diving into vibrant
underworld, I see giant
sea green turtles, grazing
on aquamarine grass and slow-dancing
with the musical ocean.
The whitetip reef shark lurks
under a sea cave labyrinth.
Below my snorkeling eyes
drifts a cloud of hammerhead sharks
murkily in and out of sight.
I swim in awe with marine iguanas
as black as the mangroves
into the turquoise tide.

This is an exotic sanctuary
of Earth's well-being, revealing
Darwin's natural selection
in prehistoric galore
like a geographical cartoon.
Truly, I feel gratitude
for the Galapagos tortoise
being a spirit guide on my journey
exploring this primitive dreamscape
where nature is the storybook of life.

Rapa Nui "Easter Island"

Far, far away in Polynesian winds
an island's mystery glows
upon green shadowlands, where
extinct volcanos listen
and the sea speaks as
roaring black tides pound upon
basalt rocks of the deep past,
under marbled-blue nimbus sky
and waves of spindrift foam, lapping
upon petroglyphs and lava caves
along lonely shores.

On precipitous sea cliffs, ancient *Moai
emanate the magical power, *Mana.*
They mutely stand with strange,
enigmatic stare: penetrating the void
of existential light. Deep-slit eyes
with obsidian pupils under protruding
brow lines hide the red scoria in
dark latitudes, bewildering the compass.
On velvet green slopes, monolithic
faces eerily emerge from blue-black
tuff in stone quarry matrix.

Upon vast lava plains of grass and rocks
wild horses race through the
winds, trampling bare earth
with long manes, freely flying
above muscles, sinews and viscera
in a galloping thunder of flesh
across the treeless terrain with freedom
of primal forces, lacerating
space and time into a cosmic
dance, so eloquent that a myth
arises, spontaneously in the rhythm
of raw pursuit for past on surreal island...

*Moai - Monolithic human figures carved by the Rapa
Nui people on Easter Island 1250 – 1500

Incan Shamanic Journey Trilogy
Sacred Site/Power Animal/Consciousness

1. Necropolis/Serpent/Subconscious

Somewhere, in nocturnal jungle
the sun rays sear through a canopy hole,
enlightening a dark constellation:
I follow the serpent's trail, slithering
a disturbed pattern of silence
along the nether river, submerged
in a cave of black diamonds
and subterranean catacombs.
Sacred diversity in Amazon jungle
with infinite shades of green
and necromantic endeavors
disguises as owl's eye wings,
in intricate thickets of verdure
with spider webs across the path
and fire ants on a holy tree
as symbiotic alliances,
with harlequins beneath the surface.
There is no enclave for a rose
on the incumbent wings of death
with strangler figs and anacondas
hidden in gnarled mists of forests
amidst the humid, malarial breeze
camouflaging into still vortex
as portal for the Shaman's Journey,
guiding spirits through a serpentine
underworld to a subconscious prelude
of the past. I listen to occult whispers
from consciousness, profound
enough to find:

the primal instinct craves a journey
intertwined in ayahuasca vines,
instead of shallow wanderlust afar,
excavating a hollow of death
and deep penetrating winds
for transformation into oracle of bright stars.

2. Cusco/Puma/Conscious

Midway between high desert
and jungle's exotic umbrage,
the Inca pathways radiate
triumphantly from Temple of the Sun.
An empire of gold and blood
aligned with a star stream
as Milky Way's celestial river
flowing to nourish *Pachamama
into gilded quadrants of power.
I listen to the ancestors
of Andean zampona, interplayed
between pipes of sun and moon
haunting the Andes with a song, longing
for diverse people as one.

Quechua symbols sing
in colorful textile designs
with a spectrum of lyrics.
Tapestries unfold myths, stories
and deities with delicate threads
into themes of valor.
Purple mountain swaths of
blue trees, green sky and
white earth weave

with blood-stained clouds.
A mosaic lake of raindrops
reflects crystal moonlight
in metallic dreamscapes from a loom.

Huacas' processional landmarks
of rocks, trees, and sacred mountains
are stellar for rituals and sacrifices,
wearing talismans of night sky.
The cloth rainbows, coral shells
and macaws' bright feathers
feed a patina of brass fire
in sacred, ambrosial glow.

My arcana of coca leaves...
beckoned by omens in wind
blow auspiciously through divine air,
falling on brown earth
in mystical shapes as an oracle
for maestro's storytelling.

Upon high plateau, the citadel
is *Sacsayhuaman, sculptured
with limestone into puma's skull,
in cyclopean masonry and
jaws of megalithic muse.
It lacerates with supernatural precision
the heart's interlocking stones,
as stronghold to survive centuries
of earthquakes, wars and carnage.
Eclectic array of colossi
show eternal glory...

I walk this earth with the
puma's paws, peripatetic,
male and female forces as symbiotic
gravitation to love…
emerged from Lake Titicaca
gleaning a vast cordillera, centripetal,
back to the navel, whispered in winds,
not written in Quechua language
about People of the Sun
balanced by Law of Reciprocity,
while the living and dead co-create

3. Machu Picchu/Condor/Superconscious

From dense jungle of opulent-green
canopies and secret undergrowth,
I rise above the humid stasis
to a realm where bright spirits dance
aloft, in alpine air…
nourishing the soul with ethereal winds
in azure womb of vertiginous heights.
From a harbinger of light,
I begin the healing sojourn toward sun
as a gilded mirror to condor's flight
emanating rays of awesome power.
Vastly, I feel evanescent blue
as a transparent window to heal
amidst kaleidoscope of dreams
and bright omnipotence!

Inti, God of golden sun burns
the past with fire of wisdom
blowing white smoke as

ephemera into afterlife, transported
by a condor's wings...
How elite is the sun as ultimate power?
A quandary to science and art
is a hologram of mystery,
consecrated as a magnum opus above
the supernal gardens of granite
with pink orchids dappling
soft petals in cracks.
I gaze through the palace of three windows
at the serpent, puma and condor
coalescing a trinity
into splendor as intuition of being.

Humbly, I follow labyrinth on mountaintop
along dreamscapes of wonder
in high altitude of diaphanous breeze
finding a mystic muse,
with illusions of granite as my guide.

Trapezoidal doors frame majesty
with gale alight to warm my skin
and stone steps to ground
imagination's spiritual breath.
High masons designed a matrix
to reflect the moon and stars
as interstellar geometry.
At Temple of the Moon,
silver shines in night sky
a glitter of darkness, as above
so below in lunar divination.

Spring water trickles down

terraced gardens growing
maize as bullions from the sun,
fermented into golden chicha.
Sculptures of elements
wait under condor's eyes, as
chimerical creatures crawl
to stillness on steep mountainside,
petrified and polished by the winds,
as posterity uncovers myths
for ancestors of the sun and Urubamba.

Ascent or descent on this treeless plane
with no flat, complacent ridge
or shade to forget the sun's power.
Time rests in expanse so vast that I sigh
with latitude to streamline
a clear atmosphere for thoughts to rise
amidst a draft of feather blue.

This ineffable bliss empowers
a sense of awe so intense,
that I am calm with a newfound wisdom,
enswathed by a serene wake of the past
recognizing nature on its altar:
Alone with a gust of shamans,
I imagine midair…
a realm so vast that a thousand condors fly
as a cloud of wings on ether highways
above the taciturn stones.

*Pachamama - Mother Earth in Quechua
*Sacsayhuaman- Cusco Citadel shaped like
a puma's head

Emerald Fire

EMBLAZONS
glass dreams, brilliant
in cascades of ice,

as green opulence
cuts the clear
beryl, enlightened by
bright mind

feeling the crystal
blades of grass bleed
from Colombian jungle.

North America

"Your body is not a temple,
it's an amusement park.
Enjoy the ride." - Anthony Bourdain

Ode to The Traveler
Prince Christian Sound, Greenland

The Traveler feels wildness
remote as their soul
upon moment of death
inhale raw beauty
with breath as a bridge to
sojourn of oneness…

with contours and elegance
of asymmetry, aligned
by cosmic forces and cycles
in spiral motifs, encrypted
as dream symbols,
painting elite patterns
upon clear, cold winds
into clouds of the fjord's air.

Sculptures of eons
rise into glaciated sky,
as Arctic creatures incarnate
the granite realms of solitude.
Unpretentious canyons
in simple strata's
brown, gray and black
primitive geology, recycle
nature's holograms, contrasting
white and blue icebergs
in a nonchalant flowing wing
of water and light.

Ice floes shapeshift
into frozen shadows and
deep indigo dreaming
under deluge of crystals...
drifting as lost ghosts haunting
amidst tidewater glaciers, waning
like the moon wearily
in animate rocks,
melting moments as our planet
warms the sky-blue snow
into calving explosions and
dying waterfalls...

At Greenland's Cape Farewell,
the Traveler flows alongside
icebergs on glass currents
melting into Labrador Sea...

Cemetery in Qarqotoq

In Greenland's granite fjords is a garden
of spirits. Behind light blue glacier
winds freeze forgotten grief.
The white cross is a compass
for lost angel, immortalized
by epitaph. A constellation of graves
with gold and purple wildflowers
become one steppingstone.

Death is a whisper
from the shimmering moon in
cold sky with iceberg on crest
of arctic willows, closer
to the glass realm. Bones are
the words for all prayers to bloom
at night in buried cloud.

Endangered Sea Butterfly (Pteropod)

Ultraviolet wings
quiver, vulnerably-lit

by deep dreaming
symbols…

in thready swirls
of transparent tissue

and shell, spun like
a web of bone,

dissolving sadly
into alchemy of

ocean, like the
blue death darkness,

as strange mutation
in acid blood,

shapeshifting
the ancient food chain.

Walking North Head Trail
St. John's, Newfoundland

On Signal Hill
the Atlantic winds awaken
while peripatetically, I emerge
from deep sky.

The atmosphere is pure
and indigo is electric
knowing this will
extend time…
feeling the synapsis fire
my connection to everything.

Awakened by trust,
that it's safe to open
all senses and be the
wanderlust. I feel
the elements of natural wonder, so
happiness happens
ineffably.

The wind is a carrier
of goodness to my heart.
The sun is a lantern
for my spirit.
The ground is a path
to walk with love.
The granite rock
is a steppingstone for
my soul's journey.

The infinite freshness
clears cache from my wired brain.

From the precipice, I see
majestic blue and gold horizon,
like a vision board of my dreams.
Is this a cliché for postcards or
really mine for redemption?
Turning around, surprised…
I discover a red Adirondack chair
with maritime possibilities.
Seated, I root into true self
and absorb seascape, a teardrop
in my ocean forever.

Cruising Glacier Bay, Alaska

Bewildered, I feel a deep chill
in the vastness of a water sanctuary
as supernatural mirror reflects alpine clouds
cascading color and light into sojourn.
Ice sculptures of indigo
glades shimmer raw majesty
through misty granite fjords.
Tidewater glaciers calve
into BOOM of ice, wind and waves
as *Tlingit* rainbow splashing
ancient legends from opaque elements.

Amidst a crystal gale, snow
clouds hover, hauntingly on craggy
summit casting mute shadows.
Savage beauty of bald eagle soars
over exposed seal and pup
on iceberg carved by deities.
Pristine waters glean humpback
whale fluke and wild orca fin as totems
in aquamarine, lucid dreaming
amidst soft rainforest fog.

Now, I explore freedom in
hologram of my mineral bones,
as deep tidal undulations
merging thoughts with sacred geology.
In deluge of primal light,
I surrender to beatific wonder
and let go in wind, inhaling with tingling lungs
humility as the path, connecting
this sacred, wild montage. Then,
I feel a draft to euphoria as keen
insight, from my cloud sharing
revelation of a glacier sky…

*Tlingit - Indigenous peoples for North America's Pacific
Northwest Coast

Seattle Floral Inferno

Blossoms of ash
glisten air with
iridescent smoke, lightly
as dirge for spring dalliance.

Crocus wings inflame
meadow saffron nuances of
embers and petals
from winter blues,

as daffodils dance
lithely in the
sun's shadows and golden
dawn of jasmine's

seductive fragrance
awakening portals of
memory, adolescent to the
romantic mind:

a cherry blossom's
pink esoteric language
translates the ephemera
into seeds of desire

till twilight awakens
tulip's silk corolla
muse, as bold stamens
pollinate air…

near a magnolia tree
of holographic seasons
growing gravity's rainbow,
under the cellar door.

The Ocean

sprays air w/streamed
crystal of fountain frieze.
SPINDRIFT!
The breeze
inhales blue surface
into aerial waves o'er
pools of drowning.
Cool liquid breath
of clear oxygen
w/bubbles
to rise
as the deluge
engulfs vulnerable rocks
of green moss
where an osprey circles…

Skagit Valley Tulip Festival

Effervescent fields paint emotions
with spritz of light, laughing…
as spectacle of glory happily digs
the dirt's roots and misty froth
in moment for fog and sun.
Petal dew aroma wafts
on waves of hilly horizons
as white clouds hover
the neon bulbs,
beneath my straw hat.

I follow imagination
like a kite, flailing in wind over tulips,
alongside Cascade Mountains
humbling my shy heart
on verge of awareness about
the essence of spring folly.

Hummingbird

A waft of wings
hummms gently,

hovering over grass
in soft breeze...

Heart's wingbeat
infinitely flutters

into a prismatic-
green muse.

Tufts of light
clear as calligraphic art

upon pink stem
brush a downstroke

into circular wake
vortices of air...

Oregon Pink Mists

Through misty
curtains…

a pale pink
softness of damask

roses blushes
a subtle brilliance,

in fragile fog of
a surreal dream

with pearly, silver
nuances glistening

pastel gardens.
Petals drip

fragrant dew
of morning eve.

Decadent gray
barn appears

through breath
of blue air

then vanishes
into fog of roses…

Phoenix in Santa Ana Winds

Inferno of red and gold plumes
with azure tail emblazons
me into bright gust, fanned
by wing's shadow…
Setting sun crashes
onto ridgeline, bleeding
a feverish fire
ignited by tinder pyre!

It's been 50 years and
my heart is too ancient
for the young blood spilling
on dry chaparral,
smoldering combustion
of night, enveloped by dawn.
Passionately, I transform
into infinite awareness…
amidst ashes and smoke rising
with orange embers crackling
helplessly in devil winds!
Firebrand etiquette
is unconquerable
on incendiary path of purification.

If I let go…
I won't get burned,
blazing a higher trail
as ending starts fire tornado.
There is no manmade law
to extinguish the supernatural:
Thus, I learn to dance
with fire and wind
and flow with the streams of water
upon still earth.

Barbados Shipwreck Dive

Beneath the sapphire sea time dissolves to mystery
montage, letting go in fluid elegance imagining I
am a mermaid swimming in symbolic realms
where I discover the secret treasure, while
swimming with pearls, gold & barnacled
skin, among the crystal fish, emerald
turtles and glass stingrays.   Coral
reef diversifies an infinite bloom
with transparent anemones &
red heart polyps, perilously
luring candescent shoal.
Mindstream splashes
& feels the currents
tide in flow of the
moonlit silvers
glittering my
reflections
DEEP.

Belize Black Orchid

There is an alchemical garden
where my essence grows
like a black orchid

in mists of gaping vines,
intertwined-
with a vague light

of silver moon, glowing
through vulnerable leaves
as dark insight.

A deep breeze awakens
fragrant-damp petals
of dewdrops in rainforest

inflections of purity
and auroral, raw warmth
amidst shadows of bright essence.

Death Valley, USA
Montage of Ukraine War

At Death Valley,
I first hear of Russia
attacking Ukraine. Vagrantly,
from periphery, I absorb motel news
in Mojave Desert mirage
where solo journey feels
winds of humanity, faraway,
from my hot, thirsty days
through oasis shadows…

Salt crystals shapeshift
holograms below sea level
from silent, white bomb rifts
imploding time-lapsed geology
from Black Mountains.
Beyond Furnace Creek
the valley transforms into
mesquite sand dunes
swirling smokey green into
orange horizon for prayer,
with kindness as a grain
of sand, vulnerable at noon
scorching dreams to bone
for refugees' home.

Seeking deep nature,
I wander surreal passages
at Mosaic Canyon, where
broken hearts bleed
love on to bare, sanguine rocks,

scratching souls;
meanwhile, smooth marble
glistens the child's teary
good-bye to a father,
war-torn by love.

On vacant highway
badlands erode rusty-pink
and brown waves of austerity.
Visions are somewhere
in the Artist's Palette, painting
mineral kaleidoscopes
of copper and iron hope,
with lavender-dust trails through rose
hills beneath sapphire skies.

The Devil plays
on his golf course, maligning
greed with salty spheres
into a crevasse of death.
Who is culpable for Dante's view,
I ask on the precipice of now,
while we stream online
the ash and leaden clouds?

Ultimately, I take a pilgrimage
to the Red Cathedral,
where divine canyons patiently
erode pain and suffering…
Returning, I see the Ukraine flag
lucidly at Golden Canyon,
blending into cobalt-blue sky
like a harbinger for peace…

Epiphany at Sunset Cliffs, San Diego

On a precipice
the unknown seduces me, then fades away
like an intimate dream vaguely
remembered, as I stand in stillness
and know…

the sensuous breeze
gnawing at my heart
with uneasy feeling
to let go of something
I love.

I try to imagine the wind
in a surreal light
through transparent night
whispering secrets
from the moon's shadow,

but it eludes, provocatively,
wafting air
into midnight blue
sky of silver stars, strewn
like a bewildered companion

finding clarity in constellations
designed in cosmic harmony
with the music of spheres
illuminating a destiny
that dances with divine will…

Home

The moon
is spilling
a tranquil light
into waters of a silent dream
as stillness flowing through the clear
window of death,
where love is just a mere breath of being
subtle, yet deep and powerful
as the crest of an ocean beam…
feeling a rhythm of divine inheritance
fresh like winds from a wildflower meadow
and crisp as the autumn leaves that fall in death
upon spacetime to the unknown…
where mystery is strange and beautiful
as I rise toward colors of the moon
in a transparent, blue dress
and splash of silver sequins
to a deep reservoir where tears quell
innocent passion and lustrous will,
while flames lick sweat off my moist skin
and warm into a soothing recognition
that I am home.

About the Author

"Poetry is the language of travel,
like dreams are the language of subconsious."

Trudy Wendelin is a self-taught poet, giving rise to her authentic voice for free-verse poetry. She's also an avid world traveler, exploring 100+ countries and a travel writer. *True Wind Travel Poems* is a collection of 50 poems inspired by her travels to all 7 continents.

Additionally, Trudy published a more classical book entitled *The Silver Chalice Sonnets*. She graduated from Pacific College of Health and Sciences in San Diego and is a Licensed Acupuncturist. Encouraged by the healing arts, she also wrote and co-produced the 5 Element Meditation Series of East Asian Medicine. Trudy resides in Seattle, Washington when she's not globetrotting.